Filibuster Solution

By Edward D. Campbell, J.D.

Filibuster Solution

The People's Answer to the Senate's Super Majority Rules
or
Returning the Senate to the States and the People

By Edward D. Campbell, J.D.

A workable solution that We the People can control

ISBN: 978-0-9834795-0-5

Library of Congress Registration Number TXu 1-754-841

Published by Amida Biometrics, L.L.C.
Seattle, Washington, U.S.A.
www.edcampbell.com

Dedication

This work is dedicated to all those who truly admire the Constitution of the United States and the rights and power of the States and the Citizens of each of those States.

Table of Contents

Forward

For over two hundred years it has been possible for a small number of senators to block the democratically supported will of the people of the United States by hiding behind the "rights of unlimited debate" and the Senate rule requirements of unconstitutional super-majorities. It is abundantly clear from the history of the United States Senate that the members of the Senate are totally unwilling or incapable or correcting this fault and returning the Senate to its constitutional position of being an equal representative of the States and in representing the citizens of those states as equal partners.

We provide a history of this deprivation of the constitutional guarantees of the representative form of government in the United States Senate together with a method or methods that you, the States and the citizens, can use to reassert your rights without further reliance on members of the Senate who have only proved they are not capable of correcting this denial of our constitutional representation. You can do this by reliance on the existing Constitution without any need to elect new Senators or to amend that Constitution. Share these ideas with your fellow Citizens, so that all may be informed and can take appropriate action.

I. FILIBUSTER REVOLUTION

States' Constitutionally Required Equality in the Senate

The Constitution of the United States initially declared, Article 1, Section 3:

> "The Senate of the United States Shall be composed of two Senators from Each State, chosen by the legislature thereof, for six years, and each Senator shall have one vote."

This was amended by the 17th Amendment to read:

> "The Senate of the United States Shall be composed of two Senators from Each State, elected by the people thereof, for six years, and each Senator shall have one vote."

It has always been clear that each state has only two votes in the Senate. Since the 17th Amendment, ratified May 31, 1913, the senators casting those votes have been elected by the people of those states. Thus while the power of the people throughout the United States is not equal, because of the variations of populations from state to state, the State's power's represented in the Senate has always been equal according to the plain wording of the constitution. Each state has two equal Senatorial votes except in certain matters specified in the Constitution.

Ch. 1, Filibuster Revolution

The Senate over its history has made a mockery of this obvious constitutional limitation in its practices and rules which currently continue to defy the constitution. It currently requires a 60% majority (three fifths)of the full body to bring issues before the chamber to debate and vote. These practices even allow one senator to place holds on bills and appointments. This resulted recently in Republican Minority Whip, Senator Jon Llewellyn Kyl, defying the desires of the world and threaten the safety of all nations in holding up the nuclear arms reduction treaty with Russia. That Arizona Senator almost blocked the consideration of it, the consideration of the current nuclear arms treaty. Other illustrations from the recent past are the blocking of consideration of various judicial and other appointments.

Treaties already must be approved by two thirds of the Senate, (Art. 2, §2 ¶ 2) so why should Senate rules make it easier for even a lesser number of Senators to block consideration of Treaties? Why, as we will ask again and again, should Senate Rules and practices override the provisions of the Constitution. Where in the Constitution is this right given to the Senate to change the provisions that govern that body as set forth in the Constitution?

Ch. 1, Filibuster Revolution

Mathematical Inequality in The Senate

The 60 vote requirement means that 41 votes can block any issue, any appointment, any bill in the absence of some special rule. So this means that 41 senators outweigh 59 senators. The relative weights are $41x > 59y$. The ratio of x/y is x greater than y: $59/41 = 1.44$. In this case the inverse -- y/x, is > 0.69. So when the filibuster is used in the Senate, each Senator on the side of the filibuster has the weight of at least 1.44 Senators, while those on the other side only have the weight of .69 Senators. By simple math, the states do not have equal representation in the Senate under the current rules. Instead of having one vote as required by the Constitution, Senators under Senate rules, must have more than 59 votes weighted at more than 1.44 each both to consider and pass any controversial bill or appointment. But they only need 41 votes weighted at 0.69 vote each to block any controversial measure, appointment or issue. Obviously the States do not have equal representation in the Senate.

Constitutional Inequality

The constitution does provide for unequal representation in the Senate in special cases. While the power to make treaties is granted to the President, they shall not become the law of the land until ratified by two thirds of the Senators present Art. 2 §2 ¶2. The framers considered requiring unequal representation in the Senate, but limited it

Ch. 1, Filibuster Revolution

to the consideration of Treaties; the expulsion of members by concurrence of two thirds of its members (Art. I §5 ¶2); conviction of impeached officers of the United States by two thirds of the Senators present (Art. I §3 ¶7); and to the passage of bills over the veto of the president Art. I §7 ¶2 which requires a two third majority of each house of Congress. No where was the Senate given the right to otherwise change the weight of the votes of Senators in the Constitution either by practice or rule. It is clear that the framers of the constitution considered weighted voting in the Senate. Given the fact that the constitution did consider the relative value of the weight of the votes of Senators and so limited it, how can any Senate take on to itself a right to amend the Constitution and enlarge this power, by adding new weighted voting restrictions?

In fact, the Constitution even considered weighted voting when it provided the Senate could make its own rules. Consider the full text of Article I, section 5: "Each House may determine the Rules of its Proceedings, punish its members for disorderly behavior, and, with the Concurrence of two thirds, expel a member." Only expulsion requires a super majority.

This contrast between what is expressed and what is omitted occurs within a single sentence. There is a doctrine of legislative and constitutional interpretation that failing to expressly include a power within the grant of that power, implicitly excludes it. It is very old having and the Latin

Ch. 1, Filibuster Revolution

term for this interpretive rule is *expressio unius est exclusio alterius*.

The reasoning of *expressio unius* is quite powerful. It might remain debatable whether the Constitution's seven super majority references are illustrations, instead of a complete list. But when a 2/3 super majority requirement is imposed in the same sentence for one activity but left out when referring to other activities in the same sentence, it is entirely reasonable to assume that the other activities are governed by a simply majority vote.

The Senate Rule XXII

While each house of Congress may "determine the rules of its proceedings" (Art. I §5 ¶2), the constitution does not grant either house the authority to make rules that contravene of the plain language of the constitution.

The original rules of the Senate did not allow for the filibuster because there was a rule that allowed the Senate to move the previous question, which if passed by a majority present, terminated debate and moved the bill or other issue before the Senate to a vote. No senator or minority of senators could block a bill or other action permitted by the Constitution to the Senate so long as a simple majority of the Senators present wanted to consider it.

It was argued in the early nineteenth century that this

Ch. 1, Filibuster Revolution

motion was redundant and Aaron Burr pointed out that the motion to end debate and get on with voting had been exercised only once in the previous four years. The Senate agreed and in recodifying its rules in 1806 removed this rule and provided no other rule to end debate. The groundwork for the Filibuster was laid. It is interesting to observe that under the original rule the equality of all senators was recognized as it only took a majority to end debate.

The Filibuster remained a theoretical option for about three decades until 1837 when the first attempt at interminable debate, to talk a bill to death, occurred. The Senate is a deliberative body and each Senator has unlimited time to speak twice in any legislative day on any issue before the Senate. Thus on any bill each Senator cold speak twice, as well as twice on any amendment to that bill and any amendment to any proposed amendment. The groundwork is laid for effective delaying practices in the Senate. A legislative day is not a calendar day but goes from adjournment to adjournment, thus through recesses, a legislative day may be lengthened into several calendar days. The core of the Senate practice governing floor debate is paragraph 1(a) of Senate Rule XIX:

1. (a) When a Senator desires to speak, he shall rise and address the Presiding Officer, and shall not proceed until he is recognized, and the Presiding Officer shall recognize the Senator who shall first

Ch. 1, Filibuster Revolution

address him. No Senator shall interrupt another Senator in debate without his consent, and to obtain such consent he shall first address the Presiding Officer, and no Senator shall speak more than twice upon any one question in debate on the same legislative day without leave of the Senate, which shall be determined without debate.

The first test attempt at cutting off the debate came during the consideration of the bill to charter the Second Bank of the United States in 1841. Senator Henry Clay tried to force a vote on the bill by forcing a vote on closing debate. He was opposed by Senator Thomas Hart Benton who accused him of trying to stifle debate. Benton's opposition carried the day. There was no rule for cutting off debate until a compromise was reached during the debate on the Treaty of Versailles in 1917. Then the Senate adopted Rule 22 allowing it to end debate by a two thirds majority vote of the actual Senators present. This rule was revise in 1975 when the number required for cloture was reduced from two thirds to three fifths. But rather than three fifths of the senators present, it is now three fifths of the entire body of the Senate. A vote of 60 Senators is required to end debate in a full Senate of 100. Unless the majority leader has sixty votes he cannot call for closure and expect to win. One Senator can threaten to filibuster and the majority leader must go back and count his votes to see if he has the sixty to win. The actual exercise of the filibuster is no longer even necessary. Even if the vote were reduced to a majority of the senators, or a majority of the Senators present, the threat of a filibuster is still a very serious threat of delaying the entire Senate's business.

Filibusters, Cloture and Delays

The filibuster not only poses threats of delays by Senators speaking on issues, but also delays that are inherent in trying to cut off that debate and halt the filibusters.

While the Senate no longer permits limitless time for debate, restricting it is the challenge. On inconsequential bills and those that receive by-partisan support, unanimous consent of the Senate may be reached to limit debate. Where the unanimous consent cannot be reached on issues that the Senators can filibuster, the only effective way to cut off debate is by cloture.

The opportunity to filibuster will arise at two points. First is the decision to consider a bill. This may be filibustered. A senator voting at this point does not really register his or her stand on the underlying measure considered. He or she could offer a variety of reasons for not bringing up a bill while telling the constituents that he does not oppose the measure in principal but it is not timely before

Ch. 1, Filibuster Revolution

the Senate. This is one means Senators put holds on bills, possibly for their own personal unexpressed ends. If any Senator threatens to do this, the majority leader, who must find time for all actions before the Senate, is faced with a very time consuming procedure of bringing on a cloture motion, which must be made by 16 Senators. The leader must also consider does he have 60 Senators who may or will vote for cloture. The leader cannot afford to waste time during a busy legislative session so many bills can be lost just on the threat of a filibuster. Towards the end o a Congress the leader may not even call up bill that could be filibustered because he feels the Senate's time must be devoted to other matters. One Senator representing possibly less than .2% of the population can put the national legislative agenda on hold and actually defeat important measures, or wring earmarks or other concessions for his state, political backers or personal ends.

When a cloture motion is made under rule XXII the rule imposes a cap of no more than a total thirty hours to consider it. This includes time consuming quorum calls, roll call votes, parliamentary inquiries and all other proceedings that occur while the matter under the cloture motion is pending before the Senate. The time can be extended by passing a non-debatable motion for that purpose by the three fifths majority. Before a cloture motion there is no rule that the Senate's debate has to be germane to the issue before it. A senator could read a cook book. After the cloture motion,

Ch. 1, Filibuster Revolution

the rule is that it must be germane

The Senate rules set forth time periods for consideration of cloture. Also the rules require that issues, except treaties, cannot proceed to debate until a motion to proceed is passed.

Actual Time That May Be Required for Senate Action in a Typical Cloture Situation

Senate Action	Days in Session	Calendar Days
Motion to proceed (MP)	1	1
Cloture motion on MP	1	1
Vote on MP Cloture	3	3
Vote on MP	6	8
Cloture Motion on measure	6	8
Vote on 2nd Cloture Motion	8	10
Vote on final passage of measure	11	15

It is obvious. Cloture can eat up a good part of half a calendar month unless the Senate can agree by unanimous consent to speed up the process.

If the Leader undertakes a cloture motion, he will

Ch. 1, Filibuster Revolution

consider also a cloture motion on the debate of the bill itself. The object is to save some time

The Effects of The Senate Rule

The United States is not a democracy. It is an unequal Republic. 25 of the least populous states, half of the United States, contain less that one sixth of the total population of the country.

The least populous state, Wyoming, has less than .2% of the total population of the United States and its territories. The territories account for only .32% of the population. Wyoming has two senators. Either one of them can threaten a filibuster and cripple consideration of issues or appointments before the Senate. Even if the Cloture rule were changed to allow 51% of the Senate to approve a cloture, this would still only represent about one sixth of the total population of the United States.

The most famous recent use of this dilatory practice before the two thirds rule change was the one that southern Senators unsuccessfully staged to block civil rights legislation, including anti-lynching legislation, until cloture was invoked after a 57 day filibuster against the Civil Right Act of 1964.

Ch. 1, Filibuster Revolution

Today with the three fifths rule on Cloture it takes only senators representing as little as 11.2% of the population to effectively curb consideration of any issue or appointment before the Senate. The Senate is the home of the American Oligarchy. The Senate is the Gag on American democracy. Eleven of the most populous states represent 56% of the population and have a majority in the Electoral College to elect a president, and the majority of the population can still rule in the House of Representatives. But not even a majority of the States can rule the Senate. Is this what the founders planned?

The Founding Fathers

The first place to look for what the founding fathers had in mind when they wrote the constitution is the records of the Constitutional Convention of 1787. When it came to deciding how many Senators each state would have, two or three, it was already accepted that the senators would be able to vote "per capita." This mode Mr. Oliver Elseworth [Connecticut] acknowledged in debate that he had always approved.[1] This meant that all Senators would vote on an equal basis, they would each share and share alike in the voting of the Senate. This was approved as the number of 2 Senators from each State was approved and continued to be approved into the final document.

Ch. 1, Filibuster Revolution

The next place to observe what the founding fathers had in mind when writing the constitution are the Federalist Papers, that group of essays bf James Madison, Alexander Hamilton and John Jay written in support of adoption of the Constitution. In number LXII the authors (either Madison or Hamilton dwelt for some time over the number of senators provided and why. Of particular significance is this passage:

> "In this spirit it may be remarked, that the equal vote allowed to each State is at once constitutional recognition of the portion of sovereignty remaining in the individual States, and an instrument for preserving that residuary sovereignly. So far the equality ought to be no less acceptable to the large than to the small States; since they are not less solicitous to guard, by every possible expedient, against an improper consolidation of the States into one simple republic."[2]

It is clear that the founding fathers envisioned no cloture rule requiring 60 votes for consideration of a bill or approval of any appointment or to open or close debate. That was an amendment of the constitution that the Senate achieved through adoption of special rules, a power not found in the constitution when one looks to the way it may be amended. There is nothing in the Constitution that says the Senate can amend it by changing its rules.

Ch. 1, Filibuster Revolution

The "Constitutional Option"

When Senator Robert C. Byrd (D-WV) was faced with a filibuster in 1979 on his rule change proposals he raised the possibility that the Senate could change the cloture rule at the beginning of each new Congress by a majority vote. He reasoned that as the first Congress in 1789 had only adopted those rules by a majority vote, each Senate could not bind that followed to rules restricting their actions in adopting rules by any greater:

> "The Constitution in article 1, section 5, says that each House shall determine the rules of its proceedings. Now we are at the beginning of Congress. This Congress is not obliged to be bound by the dead hand of the past.
>
> ....
>
> The first Senate, which met in 1789, approved 19 rules by a majority vote. Those rules have been changed from time to time....So the Members of the Senate who met in 1789 and approved that first body of rules did not for one moment think, or believe, or pretend, that all succeeding Senates would be bound by that Senate.... It would be just as reasonable to say that one Congress can pass a law providing that all future laws have to be passed by two-thirds vote. Any

Ch. 1, Filibuster Revolution

Member of this body knows that the next Congress would not heed that law and would proceed to change it and would vote repeal of it by a majority vote.

[I]t is my belief–which has been supported by rulings of Vice Presidents of both parties and by votes of the Senate–in essence upholding the power and tight of a majority of the Senate to change the rules of the Senate at the beginning of a new Congress."

This has become known as the constitutional option. It was first used by Senator Thomas J. Walsh (d-MT) in 1917. His opponents gave way when they realized he had the votes to carry out the option. This resulted in the Senate adopting its first formal cloture rule. In 1917, 1919, 1959, 1975 and 2011, the threat of the constitutional option induced the minority to go along with rule changes. None of these changes removed the basic flaw in the Cloture rule which is the unequal voting power of the states in the Senate in proceedings where it is not required by the Constitution.

Minor changes have been made: limitations on dilatory amendments, to propose legislative amendments to appropriation bills, to debate motions to proceed on nominations, to reduce the number of nominations that need to be confirmed, and to use tactics to delay or disrupt roll call votes or put silent holds on legislative matters. If the majority has a friendly Presiding officer, it can seek

Ch. 1, Filibuster Revolution

amendments to Standing Rules or adoption of Standing Orders by a majority with a favorable ruling from the Presiding Officer. But none of this guarantees the constitutional right of each state to be equally represented in the general business of the Senate.

Chapter 2. Cloture History, Part 1[3]

After the Senate eliminated in 1806 the rule allowing the majority to call for the previous question, thus ending debate, the Senate took no action to impose any other rule to end debate. At the time Aaron Burr thought it superfluous and he was probably right under then commonly understood parliamentary procedure. Lack of a rule to end debate did not appear to cause any problems for almost thirty years.

In 1834 the Senate had gone on record as censoring President Andrew Jackson for withdrawing deposits from the Bank of the United States. His supporters went on an unrelenting campaign to erase the censure, supported by the state legislatures in six states which replaced their Senators between 1835 and 1837. The stage was set to consider a motion to remove the censor from the Senate Journal. When the motion came up for debate, the opponents availed themselves of the Senator's unlimited time for debate and "talked and talked." Democratic Senator Thomas Hart Benton (MO) reported that "It was evident that consumption of time, delay and adjournment was their plan." Jackson's side prepared and stocked a nearby room with food and wines for a long night. Near midnight the opposition gave up and the Senate passed the resolution expunging the Jackson censorship. But the example of what might be done in debate was set.

Ch. 2, Cloture History - Part 1

This was the first mistake. But at first it only appeared as a theoretical mistake, because the Filibuster depended upon the endurance of the speaker. However, clearly the seeds of unconstitutional control of the Senate were laid in the very existence of the filibuster without a way for the majority to control it. Otherwise, if one or Senator or a few Senators could control all of the time of the Senate, then the other Senators would not have an equal voice in the business of the Senate, and the basic rule of one Senator, one vote would become useless.

The filibuster is found in other Westminister Parliamentary types of democracies and when successful the measure many have been said to be "talked out." But in the English House of Commons, unlike the United States Senate, the speaker can only cover points germane to the topic under discussion. This appears to result in shorter filibusters. To be fair to all members, time allowed for debate must take into consideration time required for the body to consider all the business before it, and needs to be apportioned, divided, appropriately to preserve the constitutional limitation of one Senator one vote.

Cloture First Considered

The first occasion to consider actually curtailing the

Ch. 2, Cloture History - Part 1

debate came during consideration of a Fiscal Bank Bill on June 21, 1841. Whig Senator Henry Clay (KY) reported this bill to the Senate. It was designed to establish a national bank, a policy that Andrew Jackson had successfully opposed. But the Democrats were in the minority. Democratic Senator John Calhoun (SC) proceeded to make it clear during the debate that the minority would not be rushed to a decision. Clay attempted to bring back the original Senate rule of calling for the previous question "to allow a majority to control the business of the Senate." Democratic Senator William King asked Senator Clay if he planned to introduce a gag measure, and Clay replied that indeed he did. King made it clear that he intended to filibuster the motion stating: "I tell the Senator, then, that he may make his arrangements at his boarding house for the winter. Clay's own supporters , fearing a breakdown of all relations, convinced him to stand down, and a compromise was reached so that a bill was passed in the Senate on July 28.

The Senate attempted four times in the nineteenth century to reach filibuster reform. Three times it tried to add the previous question to the Senate rules, 1850, 1873, and 1883. In 1890 it attempted to create a cloture precedent by majority vote. No actual cloture rule was created until 1917.

Ch. 2, Cloture History - Part 1

In 1917 with war raging in Europe, a diplomatic crisis arose challenging the United States' neutrality. On January 19th the United States intercepted a dispatch from the German Foreign Ministry to the German Mexican Ambassador. Known as the Zimmerman note, it advised the Mexican Ambassador that Germany was planning unrestrained submarine warfare in the Atlantic and this could move America to change its neutrality commitment and become a belligerent state. The ambassador was instructed to explore whether Mexico would consider a German alliance and encourage Japan to join in such an alliance and declare war on the United States. Germany would aid Mexico in regaining New Mexico, Arizona and Texas. Germany actually began unrestricted submarine warfare on February 1.

Woodrow Wilson, then Democratic President, responded by proposing the Armed Ship Bill. This permitted the American merchant vessels to arm themselves for defense against German submarine attack. It received overwhelming House support and looked to have the same level of support in the Senate. While the bill was framed to continue America's neutrality, the Republican isolationist Senator Robert La Follette and ten of his colleagues felt is was just a step toward involving the United States in the European war. So began their successful filibuster to deny a vote on the Armed Ship Bill in the 64th Congress. The term of that 64th Congress expired on March 4, 1917.

Ch. 2, Cloture History - Part 1

Wilson called the 65th Congress into special session to consider some pending nominations. The Armed Ship Bill did not appear on his agenda. But Democratic Senator Thomas J. Walsh (MT) and Republican Senator Henry Cabot Lodge (MA) and several others argued that they were not bound to only consider the nominations but could also consider rule changes. However they faced the problem that there was no Senate rule to end debate and a rule change could only occur after debate on that rule change motion. So any proposed rule change would have to survive a possible filibuster.

Senator Walsh proposed the "Constitutional option." He argued that under the Constitution, the Senate had the power to choose its governing rules or procedure by a majority vote. Rules adopted by a past Senate could not take away that right. He proposed re-adoption of all the Senate rules except Rule XXII which governed motion procedures. He then proposed an amended Rule XXII with a cloture procedure included. This, he argued, would return the Senate to traditional parliamentary procedures including allowing measures to end debate such as the motion on the previous question, giving the Senate a method to end the filibuster.

In doing this Senator Walsh was arguing against the assumption that Senate rules were continuing in force. Such an argument had not previously been made. Walsh relied on

Ch. 2, Cloture History - Part 1

the constitution Article 1, Section 5, that allows each branch of the legislature to make its own rules. He reasoned that each house had an equal right to do this. Observing the history of the House he noted that even though house rules had required, as did the Senate rules, a two thirds or larger majority to change its rules, the House considered it had no rules at the beginning of each session. Following parliamentary procedure, the House re-adopted rules and adopted new rules as it saw fit at the beginning of each new session,

While acknowledging that the Senate had not followed this practice in every new Congress in the past, there was no reason to conclude that it could not be done. Arguably there are no new sessions of the Senate as only one third of its membership is renewed every two years. So there is a continuing body always in place. Walsh pointed out that it had been argued in the past that the Joint House and Senate rules survived from Congress to Congress but that the Senate had rejected this in 1876. He argued that the Senate had neither debated or ever formally accepted the "continuing body" theory. He argued that as Article 1, section 5 applied equally to both houses of Congress, it did not support the continuing body theory. Also he observed the uniform practice of the Senate that all bills die a the end of each session of Congress. Further this continuing body theory was "at war with theory of parliamentary government the world over, whereby these bodies assembled, conducted their business and ceased to exist on the expiration of their terms.

Republican Senator Miles Poindexter (WA) was not convinced:

> "If the office of the Senator is a continuing office and does not change in any respect during the six years of his term, how [can] the body of which he is a Member...be said to have changed in that period of time. The two things, it seems to me, are indissoluble... [because] if the members of the body have exactly the same nonvarying capacity and functions during the entire period of their term,... the body which gives them that capacity and authority must continue."

To this Walsh responded that "there is a vast difference between the Members of the Senate and the Senate. Pointing out (well before Skype and internet meetings) that the Senators could not act at home, but must act in an assembled body, he argued that Poindexter had failed to make the distinction between the parts and the whole of the Senate.

Senator Walsh then examined the State legislatures with Senates and noted that Majority rule was "universal" and he submitted a list of twenty seven legislatures that adopted new rules at the beginning of their new sessions after a general election. He questions how one Senate could impose its ideas of rules on later Senates:

> "Clearly, because the people, whose representatives we are, have a right to have all measures that engage the attention of this body considered without prejudice on account of any action that may have been taken by a Senate whose course and record had made it odious, or which, for some other reason regenerated so far as it was possible to make a change. It is because the new members, coming fresh from the people, ought to have the right to be heard and be accorded the opportunity to vote in the light of information gleaned at every stage of the passage of a bill or resolution."

Walsh continued his argument that the constitutional option was fundamental do the democratic form of government. He observed that each election reflected the current sense of the people on matters that had been as well as those that were currently before Congress. In the end Walsh's arguments were never decided as the Senate moved through a committee of ten with equal members from both parties to negotiate a cloture rule, which passes 76 to 3 on March 8, 1917.

Ch. 2, Cloture History - Part 1

The 1917 rule provided that if any 16 Senators moved to close debate on any pending measure, that motion would lay on the table until the following calendar day, and after a quorum was ascertained to be present, without further debate, the presiding officer was to call for the ayes and nays. If the ayes won the vote by two thirds of the votes present, then that pending measure would be the unfinished business to the exclusion of all other business until its disposition. Debate thereafter was limited in time and scope, and delay tactics prohibited so that the measure could be called for a timely final vote. The rule required two thirds of the Senators present to end debate on measure. So if 60 were present in the Senate chamber at the time, 40 would have to vote to end yes debate. Conversely if twenty one opposed, the filibuster could continue. Clearly Senators no longer had one vote, but either less than or more than one vote depending on where they stood on any measure. There went the Constitutional mandate stated in the Original Constitution and repeated in the Seventeenth Amendment.

On May 13, 1913. the Seventeenth Amendment of the Constitution was ratified. It embodied the populism found in Teddy Roosevelt and the changes in the National political scene around and after the turn of the twentieth century. It provided for the direct election of Senators and reiterated the constitutional mandate that "each Senator shall have one vote." No longer was the Senate the private oligarchy of the States which formerly selected the Senators. Now the

Ch. 2, Cloture History - Part 1

Senators had direct responsibility to the people who elected them in each of their states. The Nineteenth Amendment guaranteeing the right to vote to women was proposed by Congress on June 5, 1918, and adopted by the States on August 26, 1920. In 1917, the Senate was facing enormous cultural and political change with a growing Women's suffrage movement that promised greater change clearly on the horizon.

Clearly the old Senate's abilities to act as a break on political and cultural change was under extreme pressure. An easily controlled oligarch was about to become far more expensive to control, even with the majority of the States still representing less than the majority of the population. Was it time for a change, a political power change that could be accomplished without a Constitutional Amendment, through little known or understood Senate rules of procedure? Was it time for a change to reestablish the strength of the oligarchic control of the Senate that the Seventeenth Amendment had sought to remove? We leave that question to those enamored by conspiratorial theories of history and rely on the Senate's honesty and the Senators' demonstrated failure, from 1917 to the present, to understand basic first grade math on observing weights and measures. In the United States Senate 2 + 2 votes can equal three, four or five depending on who is counting for what purpose.

Chapter 3, Cloture History, Part 2

The first major change to the Cloture rule occurred with the passage of the Wherry Amendment on March 17, 1949. This resulted from the success of a clever parliamentary ruling adopted by Senate president pro temporary Arthur Vandenburg ®-MI) that the minority could avoid any filibuster cloture motion by proceeding to unlimited debate on the motion to proceed to consider a measure Senator Vandenburg reasoned that was not consideration of a measure as specified in the original cloture rule but only a consideration of a motion to proceed to consideration measure. Under this ruling, debate on such motions could not be terminated. A year later, Democratic Vice President Alvin Barkley, on March 10, 1949, reversed this ruling but his reversal was appealed and overturned by the full Senate.

Further deadlock was avoided by adoption of a compromise offered by Senator Kenneth Wherry (R-NE) that offered to broaden the cloture rule to cover motions to proceed, except for motions to proceed to consider motions for rule changes. The super majority voting requirement was raised from two-thirds of the members present, to two thirds of all Senators. Nominations were now also covered by the new rule, even though not mentioned in the debates on the rule change. Of course some conspiratorial theorists might

Ch. 3, Cloture History, Part 2

cease on this silence as further evidence of dark motives but more reasoned authors speculate that it just happened without any thought, almost by oversight,[4] confirming the lack of foresight or stupidity of the members of the Senate. The new rule became known as the "gravedigger" for any civil rights legislation.[5]

Answering the continual frustration of filibusters blocking civil rights legislation, a group of Northern Democrats and moderate Republicans resorted at the opening of the 83rd Congress in n 1953 and later at the 85th Congress in 1957 to ease the cloture requirements. Senator Clinton P. Anderson (D-NM) moved to implement the "constitutional option" but both were tabled by votes of 70 to 21 and 55-38 respectively. However the 1959 Senate included eighteen freshman Democrats. If they voted as liberals, Anderson believed he had the votes to carry out the option. He also had an advisory opinion of Vice President Richard M. Nixon that appeared to endorse the constitutional option.

However then Senate Majority leader, Lyndon B. Johnson (D-TX) opposed the move and as the majority leader he had the right to introduce the first proposal. That proposal was to push through a compromise resolution. That proposal said cloture on a measure could be achieved by a two-thirds majority of Senators present (not of the whole Senate). It also included language purporting to resolve the continuing

Ch. 3, Cloture History, Part 2

Senate controversy: "The rules of the Senate shall continue from one Congress to the next Congress unless they are changed as provided in these rules." Thus a 67 vote to revise would be needed. Johnson's compromise passed 72 to 22.

Further actions were sponsored by liberal Senators to reduce the two thirds majority to the current three fifths in the 1960's and early 1970's. This started after a two month filibuster of civil rights legislation from February 15 to April 11, 1960 that included a 157 hour and 26 minute around the clock session. After that both parties placed filibuster reform in their platforms. After much debate and maneuvering success was achieved in 1975 in the 94th Congress.

In 1975 the filibuster opponents noted that the number of Filibusters was more common than three years previously and observed the Senate legislation change from a one tract procedure requiring those who would filibuster to hold the floor virtually without interruption and rest, and thus hold up all Senate business to the newer two tract system that allowed for consideration of other legislation while the filibuster was theoretically still in progress. So filibustering was much less strenuous or irksome to fellow Senators who may have had other business that they wanted to consider.

Senators Walter Mondale (D-MN) and James Pearson (R-KS) announced they were invoking the Constitutional

Ch. 3, Cloture History, Part 2

Option on January 14, 1975. Pearson's motion would have reduced cloture to a vote of a simple majority. The Senate actually went on record three times in 1975 supporting the "Constitutional option." After much debate and many procedural moves a compromise was reached on March 7th amending rule XXII to allow cloture by three fifths of all Senators duly chosen ans sworn and not merely of those present, as Pearson and Mondale had proposed.

Filibuster Successes

The filibuster proved to be of great success to social change. The civil rights legislation was continually blocked by a minority of Senators Bills to protect black voters were talked to death in 1890. Anti-lynching bills were killed in 1922, 1935 and 1938. Anti-poll tax measures fell to filibusters in 1942, 1944 and 1946 and anti-race discrimination bills were sidetracked on eleven occasions between 1946 and 1975.[6] In 1957 Senator Strom Thurmond (D-SC)[7] was able to claim the record for the longest individual filibuster speech of twenty four hours and eighteen minutes, until his doctor required him to cease for health reasons out of concern for his kidneys. Civil rights legislation that easily passed the House of Representatives was repeatedly defeated or watered down by opposing Southern Democrats and conservative Republicans.

Ch. 3, Cloture History, Part 2

The most popular twenty four hour fictional filibuster was that conducted by a young Jimmy Stewart, playing Senator Jefferson Smith in Frank Capra's 1939 film *Mr. Smith Goes to Washington*. Famous real life filibusters have included those in the 1930's of when Senator Huey P. Long (D-LA) effectively used the filibuster against bills that he thought favored the rich over the poor or favored appointments to federal jobs for his political opponents. The Louisiana Senator would entertain listeners with his recitation of Shakespeare and his reading of recipes for "pot-lickers." He once held the Senate floor for 15 hours. Wayne Morris (I-OR) set a record on April 24, 1953. He advanced the populist cause in a filibuster of the Tidelands Oil bill that he concluded after 22 hours and 26 minutes. He had broken the 18-hour record set in 1908 by his intellectual icon, Senator Robert M. La Follette, Sr. (R-WL.). This new record stood until surpassed by Senator Strom Thurmond (D-SC).

The filibuster cloture rule has become an increasingly popular political tool. According to the Senate congressional record, there were 128 cloture motions in the 110th congress, from January 2007 through July 2008. It got far worse. The previous record since the early 70's was the 103rd and 104th Congress, with 80 and 82 motions respectively.

Ch. 3, Cloture History, Part 2

		Senate Action on Cloture Motions		
Congress	Years	Motions Filed	Votes on Cloture	Cloture Invoked
112	2011-2012	2	1	1
111	2009-2010	136	91	63
110	2007-2008	139	112	61
109	2005-2006	68	54	34
108	2003-2004	62	49	12
107	2001-2002	71	61	34
106	1999-2000	71	58	28
105	1997-1998	69	53	18
104	1995-1996	82	50	9
103	1993-1994	80	46	14
102	1991-1992	60	48	23
101	1989-1990	38	24	11
100	1987-1988	54	43	12
99	1985-1986	41	23	10
98	1983-1984	41	19	11
97	1981-1982	31	30	10
96	1979-1980	30	20	11
95	1977-1978	23	13	3
94	1975-1976	39	27	17
93	1973-1974	44	31	9
92	1971-1972	23	20	4
91	1969-1970	7	6	0
90	1967-1968	6	6	1
89	1965-1966	7	7	1
88	1963-1964	4	3	1
87	1961-1962	4	4	1
86	1959-1960	1	1	0
85	1957-1958	0	0	0
84	1955-1956	0	0	0
83	1953-1954	1	1	0
82	1951-1952	0	0	0
81	1949-1950	2	2	0
80	1947-1948	0	0	0
79	1945-1946	6	4	0
78	1943-1944	1	1	0
77	1941-1942	1	1	0
76	1939-1940	0	0	0
75	1937-1938	2	2	0
74	1935-1936	0	0	0
73	1933-1934	0	0	0
72	1931-1932	2	1	0
71	1929-1930	1	0	0
70	1927-1928	1	0	0
69	1925-1926	7	7	3

68	1923-1924	0	0	0
67	1921-1922	1	1	0
66	1919-1920	2	2	1
Total		1260	922	403

Here is a summary from AmericaBLOG on the legislation that Republicans filibustered in 2008 as an indication of what has been done:

The Emmitt Till Unsolved Crimes bill – Which would help heal old wounds and provide the Department of Justice and the FBI tools needed to effectively investigate and prosecute unsolved civil rights era-murders.

The Runaway and Homeless Youth bill -- Which would provide grants for health care, education and workforce programs, and housing programs for runaways and homeless youth.

The Combating Child Exploitation bill – Which would provide grants to train law enforcement to use technology to track individuals who trade child pornography and establish an Internet Crimes Against Children Task Force.

Note: CCE is Senator David "I Like Hookers" Vitter's bill to fight child porn which Republicans just filibustered.

The Christopher and Dana Reeve Paralysis Act – Which would enhance cooperation in research, rehabilitation and quality of life for people who suffer from paralysis.

Ch. 3, Cloture History, Part 2

Coburn put a hold on every single one, and the GOP filibustered the omnibus containing them, in addition to all of these bills which belong to actual Republicans:

Senator Thad Cochran - **Stroke Treatment and Ongoing Prevention Act** (S. 999/HR 477)

Sen. Christopher S. Bond - **Vision Care for Kids Act** (HR 507/S. 1117)

Sen. Sam Brownback - **Prenatally and Postnatally Diagnosed Conditions Awareness Act** (S. 1810/HR 3112)

Sen Domenici, Pete V - **Mentally Ill Offender Treatment and Crime Reduction Reauthorization and Improvement Act** (S. 2304/HR 3992)

Sen Lugar, Richard G. - **Reconstruction and Stabilization Civilian Management Act** (HR 1084/S. 613)

Sen Coleman, Norm - **Torture Victims Relief Reauthorization Act** (HR 1678/S. 840)

Note: The irony of Norm Colman's bill is obvious, given that the United States tortures prisoners.

Sen Stevens, Ted - **Ocean Exploration, Mapping & Research** (HR 1834/HR 2400/S. 39)

Sen Snowe, Olympia J. - **Integrated Coastal and Ocean Observation System Act** (S. 950/HR 2342)

Sen Voinovich, George V. - **Appalachian Regional**

Ch. 3, Cloture History, Part 2

Development Act Amendments of 2008 (S. 496)

It only got worse in 2009-2010. It got so bad that some Senate Democrats threatened to use the "constitutional option" at the beginning of the 112th Congress on the opening day in January, 2011. This still only remains a theory and would depend on whether Vice President Joe Biden would recognize the Senate as starting anew each two years and momentarily reverting to parliamentary Rules on the first day of the new Senate when 51 votes in the 100 member quorum would prevail in changing the rule instead of another provision in the Senate Rules. Rule XXII by its terms provides that any motion to amend the Senate Rules requires the agreement of two thirds present and voting. If all 100 Senators are present, 67 votes would thus be needed. So it can take much more to amend the rule than is needed to pass a cloture motion (60 in a 100 member Senate).

Of course, all of these unequal past and current Senate procedural rules are part of a shell game, a game of misdirection. The constitutional objections are limited to one day every two years. How clever. Neither the Senate nor the Media has to consider any constitutional objections except in early January on uneven numbered years. Even then they do not have to consider the real constitutional question but

Ch. 3, Cloture History, Part 2

whether the Vice President (President of the Senate) can declare that each Senate on that date is a new Senate and not a continuing Senate and therefore can consider new rules by a majority vote, rather than rule changes by a two thirds majority vote. This could well be characterized as staging a piece of political theater by misdirection. In 2011 it was not completed on the first calendar day, as the Majority Leader recessed the Senate on that date to be called back later in January when the Senate was adjourned for the day without any change in the cloture rule. The Republicans had completely opposed changes, and the Democrats, perhaps fearing soon becoming the minority, backed off and allowed the rule change momentum to die.

On January 27, 2011 Majority Leader Harry M. Reid(D-Nev.) and Minority Leader Mitch McConnell (R-Ky.), appearing together on the chamber floor at noon, announced the results of the latest Senate Rule 22 shell game reform. The Senate left intact the minority's right to block some legislation by requiring a 60-vote threshold through a threatened filibuster. But the leaders made a gentleman's agreement to reduce or avoid some of the decades-old stalling tactics of secret holds - where an anonymous Senator could slow action on a bill - and the delay tactic found in the ability to force amendments to be read in their entirety on the floor.

Ch. 3, Cloture History, Part 2

They also agreed to reduce to reduce by one-third the number of federal government positions requiring Senate confirmation. These currently total more than 1,200, from the secretaries of defense and state to the part-time directors of the Broadcasting Board of Governors. Both Reid and McConnell agreed that the fundamental principle of requiring a super-majority - 60 votes - to pass a bill must not be touched. In the end the Senate agreed to ban secret holds and to waive, under certain circumstances, the forced reading of amendments. They also agreed that several hundred mid-level executive-branch positions would no longer require Senate confirmation.

So we have no effective change (again) by the Senate in the Cloture rule, and no evidence that either party can count or understand the basic principles of weights and measures except when it is to some small oligarchic advantage. It is, after ninety four years or experience since 1917, clearly impossible to seek any correction action on this rule from members of the Senate that complies with the mandates of the Constitution: one senator, on vote, nothing more or less. If it takes 60 senators to bring a measure or a nomination to a final vote in the Senate, then clearly one senator does not have one vote in a hundred member Senate. It is a shell game and the Republican, Democratic and

Ch. 3, Cloture History, Part 2

Independent Senators are the Shills.

Senator Tom Harkin (D-IA), a long-time advocate of filibuster reform, is described as the lone senior senator to publicly align himself with Sens. Tom Udall (D-NM) and Jeff Merkley (D-OR) in their effort to change the Senate's rules. Under the current circumstances, Harkin is reported to have given up hope that the Senate will ever reassess itself, and is looking to the courts to step in and shake things up.

"It's clear now that the Senate can not change its rules," Harkin told me in an interview Thursday evening. "It can not." While admitting that there's a strong chance that the courts would refuse to hear a case like this, Harkin is reported to believe the courts can consider these rules. "Most people would say, well the courts won't handle it because it's a political question. But I think in this instance it's more than a political question -- it's a Constitutional question," he said. "I'm looking at that. I'm working on some things right now. But I wanted to do this first obviously to see whether or not it was still possible. I don't think it's possible."[8]

Chapter 4 - Senate Alternative Solutions

With repeated defeats of the cloture rule reform over the past century, what can be done? Senator Tom Harkin (D-IA) has suggested going to the courts but admits that there's a strong chance that the courts would refuse to hear a case like this. But Harkin believes the issue is justiciable. "Most people would say, well the courts won't handle it because it's a political question. But I think in this instance it's more than a political question -- it's a Constitutional question," he said.[9] We agree and believe there are at least 50 persons in the United States, perhaps more, who are not United State Senators, who have standing to sue and could force this issue before the courts. But before we consider that, let us consider some further suggested alternatives that might be applied in the Senate under its standing rules.

Before we expand on the options offered by this paper let us further explore Senate experience. A review of the Senate history reveals some other methods of limiting debate than the constitutional option, requirements of Rule XXII and successful unanimous consent motions.

Ch. 4 - Senate Alternative Solutions

The 1890 Aldrich Plan to End Debate

Before cloture rules were established the Republicans were faced with a filibuster of southern Democrats in 1890 on the proposed Federal Election Bill authorizing the Federal Government to oversee federal elections in the South and, it necessary, to use military enforce black voting rights. The Republicans had no cloture rule and had failed to physically exhaust the filibustering Senators. Senator Nelson Aldrich (R-RI) devised a plan to terminate the debate. He proposed to introduce a motion to close debate:

> When any bill, resolution, or other question shall have been under consideration for a considerable time, it shall be in order fora any Senator to demand that the debate thereon be closed. On such demand no debate shall be in order, and pending such demand no other motion, except one motion to adjourn, shall be made...[10]

The plan was then, that after some debate on his motion, Aldrich would "make a point of order that debate had gone far enough and that an immediate vote should be had."[11] The Republicans expected that this point of order would be

Ch. 4 - Senate Alternative Solutions

overruled by the Vice President because it had no foundation in the Senate Standing Rules. They would appeal this ruling and that appeal would call for a non-debatable decision subject to an immediate Senate vote. A simple majority could then reverse the Vice President and carry Aldrich's point of order. This would then force an immediate vote on ending the debate. The clever plan was, like the constitutional time bomb, never completed nor taken past the first step as the Democrats worked behind the scenes to sidestep the bill and move on to other subjects by a vote of 35 to 34 on January 26, 1890.

The 1977 Bryd Rule XXII Revision

The late Senator Robert C. Byrd (D-WV) proved to be a wily crow when he outmaneuvered the petrochemical delay specialists in 1977 as he settled a precedent to fix a loophole in Rule 22 as it then existed permitting continued filibusters even after a successful cloture vote. Cloture had been successfully invoked against a filibuster to a bill to deregulate natural gas. This limited each Senator to one hour of debate and prohibited any "dilatory amendment, or amendment not germane." Senators Howard Metzenbaum (D-OH0 and James Abourezk (D-SD), pursuing their delay tactics, sought

Ch. 4 - Senate Alternative Solutions

to circumvent cloture by proposing a great number of amendments, without debating them and thus preserving their time for debate (one hour per each amendment). Delay was further planned in forum and quorum calls on each amendment. The use of points of order to limit this plan would not solve the problem because even though the chair could decide the points of order without debate, his decision could be appealed by the minority to the full Senate and that ruling could be debated. The rules are cleverly written so that the skilled parliamentarian does not need enough votes to block cloture to stall debate and the Senate's business. If a motion were made to table the appeal, then the filibustering Senators would require a roll call vote to further delay. By October 3, 1977 these procedures had cost the Senate 13 days and one night in debating the natural gas bill. This included 121 roll calls and 34 live quorums.

Majority leader Robert Byrd devised and used a new plan. Previously the Chair (in this case the Vice President) would not rule on a procedural defect until requested to do so by a point of order. But Senator Byrd suggested otherwise:

"I make the point that when the Senate is operating under cloture the Chair is required to take the

Ch. 4 - Senate Alternative Solutions

initiative under Rule XXII to rule out of order all amendments which are dilatory or which on their face are out of order."[12]

Vice President Walter Mondale sustained Byrd's point of order:

> "The point of order is well taken. The Chair will take the initiative to rule out of order dilatory amendments which, under cloture, are not in order..., and which on their face are out of order."[13]

Senator Abourezk remonstrated that Byrd was attempting "to change the entire rules of the Senate during the heat of a debate ... on a majority vote"[14] and appealed Mondale's ruling.[15] the Majority leader responded with a motion to table the appeal which carried by a vote of 79-14.[16] So a majority of the Senate had changed the rule without changing the text of Rule XXII. Senator Byrd used this new precedent to call up the other procedurally defective amendments filed by Senators Metzenbaum and Abourezk. The Vice President ruled immediately that the amendments were out of order and before Metzenbaum and Abourezk could appeal, the Senator Byrd exercised his Majority

Ch. 4 - Senate Alternative Solutions

Leader's right of preferential recognition to call up the next amendment. He called up thirty three amendments in quick succession to foreclose all appeals and the filibuster was broken.[17] So some Senators with the right seniority, when assisted by a favorable Vice President, can shorten the Filibuster under the cloture rules and Byrd established a new way to do this. This further emphasizes how much the Senate is an "old boys" playground.

1980 Byrd Precedent Further Changes Rule XXII

The Senate considers matters under various calendars. Legislation is considered under the legislative calendar and treaties and nominations are considered under the Senate's Executive Calendar. Prior to 1980 precedent had determined that when a motion was made to go into executive session, as it was non-debatable it would automatically place the first treaty before the Senate. Any motion to proceed to any other Executive matter would be debatable. Wily Byrd faced a problem, as he backed the confirmation of Robert E. White as Ambassador to El Salvador. If he moved to proceed to that consideration after making the non-debatable motion to

Ch. 4 - Senate Alternative Solutions

convene and Executive session, he faced a double filibuster, one on the motion to proceed to consideration confirmation of the Ambassadorial appointment and one on the appointment itself. He set out to shorten the process and on March 5, 1980 proposed:

> "Mr. President, I move the Senate to go into executive session to consider the first nomination on the Executive Calendar."[18]

Senator Jesse Helms (R-NC) took exception under a point of order:

> "The Senator can move to go into executive session but he cannot under the rules specify what we shall consider. The Senate determines its order of business in executive session only after going into executive session. It is not in order to determine the order of executive business while in legislative session."[19]

The Vice President sustained Senator Helms point of order following Rule XXII paragraph 1 and precedents that only a motion to go into executive session was in order. Senator Byrd appealed the ruling from the Chair. He

Ch. 4 - Senate Alternative Solutions

argued there was no logical reason to distinguish between motions to proceed to nominations or to treaties.[20] Senator James McClure ®-ID) countered that the proper method was to use the requirements of Rule XXII for amending the rules and "not simply by changing the rules by a majority vote to meet a particular situation..." He urged affirming the Chair's ruling.[21]

Senator Byrd won, almost along party lines, by the Senate rejecting the Chair's ruling 38-54.[22] With this precedent motions to proceed to nominations are no longer debatable. Of course, the nominations remain debatable.

Other Simple Majority Changes Without Rule Language Change

By well planned parliamentary procedures there are other evidences that the Senate could change rules by a simple majority by changing the precedent for the meaning of those rules, without needing the super-majority for actually amending the rules. Senator Byrd proved especially adroit. In 1979 he led a group of Senators in a precedent making move to change the way appropriations bills could be

Ch. 4 - Senate Alternative Solutions

considered under Rule XVI without amending the text while considering a Defense appropriations bill. This he did by a simple majority tabling an appeal of Senator William Armstrong (R-CO) against q Chairs ruling that contradicted the plain language of the rule. Byrd won on an almost party line vote, 44-40.[23]

In 1987 Senator Byrd again faced overcoming delay tactics that required changing Senate procedure contrary to the plain text to a Standing Senate Rule, Rule XII. During a Defense authorization bill the minority invoked Tule XII requiring a roll call and that if any senator were to decline to vote when called, he or she must give the reason for his or her action and the presiding officer must submit a non-debatable question to the Senate on whether the Senator shall be excused from voting. A roll call vote arose over Senator Byrd's motion to approve the Journal, Senator John Warner (R-CA) declined to vote saying he had not read the Journal. Before a vote could be had on whether to excuse Senator Warner, Senator Dan Quale ®-IN) declined to vote and during a vote on excusing Senator Quale, Senator Steve Symms ®-ID0 declined to vote. So there were now four votes pending before the Senate, Bryd's original motion and three senators declining to vote. It appeared to be looking

Ch. 4 - Senate Alternative Solutions

into two opposite mirrors with little end in sight. Senators are not inexperienced in causing delay.

Senator Byrd procedurally worked through this by using the point of order and a series of votes along party lines to establish three precedents that radically changed voting procedures under Tule XII without revising the rule, based upon findings that such tactics as described here were out of order as dilatory tactics and though a Senator might have the right to explain his reasoning for not voting, he needed to do it concisely and not use it as a further delay tactic.[24] Senator Alan Simpson (R-WY) said that this precedent could constrain debate even when the Standing Rules appeared to prohibit such an outcome.[25]

The use of Standing Orders offer another avenue to potentially exercise the Senate's constitutional rule making powers to alter the application of Senate rules and precedents governing conference reports. These changes may be made by unanimous consent or legislatively enacted by the Senate and can alter the application of Senate cloture rules and precedents on conference committee reports; the report of the House - Senate conference committees successful efforts to resolve differences in related bills which can then, if ratified,

Ch. 4 - Senate Alternative Solutions

become law upon signature of the President.

Rule XXVIII provided in 1996 that conference committees , when issuing a conference report "shall not insert in their report matter not committed to them by either House."[26] This could be enforced by a point of order...against the report, and if the point of order is sustained, the report is rejected or shall be recommitted to the committee of conference if the House of Representatives has not already acted thereon."[27] Twice the Senate has considered this precedent, first altering it and then later reversing itself to re-adopt it by a corrective standing order.

So there are circumstances wherein the Senate can act by a majority even when the rules seem to require a super majority. But as recent action in the Senate has demonstrated, this is at best the exception, not the rule. The cloture rules still protect the need for a super majority for most major action by the Senate, clearly in contravention to the Constitution that requires two votes for each state and one vote for each Senator.

Chapter 5, The People's Solution

Senator Tom Harkin (D-IA) suggested the people's solution but did not explain what the public might do. We do not have to wait almost another century to take action to cure the uneven voting power in the Senate, or even await any further action taken by Senators. It is in the power of the people of the United States, through their states, to resolve the problem once and for all. This must be done in Federal Courts as the suit would be against the United States Senate.

Attorney Generals May Sue

The first question is who can do this besides United States Senators who have proved over the last century they are not up to the task? To bring a lawsuit, a party must have sufficient interest in the case to be regarded as a proper party. Historically this would have required a showing of personal harm though the complained of action. So immediately one can name fifty "persons" who have standing to sue on the current Senate rules that deny the States and the people of those States equal representation in the United States Senate. Each State, represented by its highest legal officer, has standing to sue. Under the Constitution the States, and the electors of each State, are entitled to Senators with equal powers in the Senate. The Attorney Generals of each state

Ch. 5, The People's Solution

who has a Senator who has been forced to respond to a cloture motion requiring a super-majority would have standing to sue. Each such State has suffered direct damage by enforcement of the Senate super-majority rules that deny equal representation and each should have standing to sue to enjoin, to block, the future application of such rules, precedents and procedures.

Can voters Sue?

The interesting question is: Should all the State Attorney Generals prove to squeamish to take action, could the people or representatives of the people take such an action? Just the possibility of this should motivate at least some Attorney Generals to take action. An argument could be made that a group, such as the League of Women Voters or other group of concerned voters, of a particular state, would have standing to sue to enforce the constitutional mandate that the Senate be represented by Senators with equal voting and representation rights, as the Seventeenth Amendment gave the selection of these Senators to the people and gave the electors a direct stake in their Senator' constitutionally guaranteed rights.

The idea that one needed standing to bring a suit is a

Ch. 5, The People's Solution

doctrine developed chiefly in the twentieth century, and can related to the Judicial clause of the constitution Article III Section 2. Current judicial doctrine might be dated from 1911,[28] but received its expression in 1923.[29] In *Frothingham v. Mellon* in 1923 the Supreme Court considered the challenge of a taxpayer to the Congressional decision to allocate funds for assistance to mothers and newborn children. The Supreme Court observed that the taxpayer had suffered no tangible injury that would confer standing to object to the expenditure. The court found that the plaintiff as a taxpayer suffered no particular injury by reason of how Congress decided to spend the revenues once collected and became public property. The Court then declined to decide "abstract questions which do not appreciably or practically affect' a plaintiff who alleges such minor and unredressable harm, that is, harm shared "in common with people generally...." *Frothingham* required plaintiffs to show the harm they suffered is unique compared to the harm suffered by all citizens that stem from the same public policy.

Here is an answer to that objection to a voter suit. The electors of State Y would be deprived of their unique powers, suffer unique harm, as electors as each state has different size populations and the powers of electors in state Y are not the same as electors in state X so any Senate rule that reduces

Ch. 5, The People's Solution

the power of State Y's Senators is not equal to that shared by all electors in the United States. Not all Senatorial electoral votes are equal across the United States, but are measured uniquely according to the State in which the voter is located and registered to vote.

We may say there are two questions of standing, the common law "prudential standing" and the constitutionally required standing under Article III, Section 2. The Constitutional standing is clear as this is arising under the Constitution and Laws of the United States. Prudential standing has nothing to do with whether the case involves a justiciable controversy. It is only concerned with whether the party is qualified to bring the suit.

In 1965 the courts moved away from the requirement in standing that the party must have some economic interest in the case. In *Scenic Hudson Preservation Conference v. Federal Power Commission the Second Circuit*[30] held that it was not necessary to show an economic interest to satisfy the case or controversy requirements under Article III §2 and this was confirmed five years lated by the Supreme Court opinion in *Data Processing Association v. Camp* holding that damage to aesthetic, conversational and recreational" interests would suffice, would merit standing.[31] This was broadened even

Ch. 5, The People's Solution

further in *United States v. Students Challenging Regulatory Agency Procedures (SCRAP)*[32] that appeared to hold that damage or threatened damage to even an identifiable trifle is enough for standing would be enough for standing. Later rulings in the environmental fields narrowed this approach but it appears to have been broadened in Justice Ginsberg's opinion for the court in the 7-2 decision in *Friends of the Earth v. Laidlaw* on 2000.[33] The trial court had found no "no concrete and particularized injury" but, in light of *Lujan v. Defenders of Wildlife*[34] (1992) and ruled that the absence of such injury did not bar the lawsuit.

The Court Precedent for Victory!

While there is no direct precedent for legal action against the super majority rules of the Senate, there is collateral precedent arising from the case of *United States v. Ballin*[35] decided on February 29, 1892. During the first hundred years of its existence, the House of Representatives did not pass legislation unless a full quorum of the House approved the bill. This promoted a clever delay tactic of not voting when the bill was called and if enough congressmen did not vote, no quorum was established and thus the bill was not approved even though a majority of those present voted for it. This practice was terminated by a new set of House

Ch. 5, The People's Solution

rules adopted in February, 1890. The New Rule XV established that a quorum is satisfied if a majority of the members are present. Congressmen withholding their votes could not destroy the quorum necessary to conduct business. The Supreme Court observed that Article 1 §5, ¶ 1 of the Constitution says "a majority of each [house] shall constitute a quorum to do business." Rule XV provided the House a cleaqr method to determine the presence of a quorum.

The Court then observed that the universal default parliamentary procedural rule is that a majority of the quorum may take action and therefore a majority of the quorum present when the vote taken was sufficient to pass the act.

Mr Justice David Joseph Brewer speaking for the Court observed:

> The constitution empowers each house to determine its rules of proceedings. It may not by its rules ignore constitutional restraints or violate fundamental rights, and there should be a reasonable relation between the mode or method of proceeding established by the rule and the result to be attained. But within these limitations all matters of method are open to the

Ch. 5, The People's Solution

determination of the house, and it is no impeachment of the rule to way that some other way would be better, more accurate, or even more just. It is no objection to the validity of a rule that a different one has been prescribed and in force for a length of time. The power to make rules is not one which once exercised is exhausted. It is a continuous power, always subject to be exercised by the house, and, within the limitations suggested, absolute and beyond the challenge of any body or tribunal.[36]

So was a quorum present? Mr. Justice Brewer continues:

> The constitution provides that a majority of each [house] shall constitute a quorum to do business. In other words, when a majority are present the house the house is in a position to do business. Its capacity to transact business is then established, created by the mere presence of a majority, and does not depend upon the disposition or assent or action of any single member or fraction of the majority present. All that the constitution requires is the presence of a majority, and when that majority are present the power of the house arises.[37]

Ch. 5, The People's Solution

But how can the quorum be determined? Mr. Justice brewer continues:

> The constitution has prescribed no method of making this determination, and it is within the competency of the house to prescribe any method which shall be reasonably certain to ascertain the fact. It may prescribe answer to roll-call as the only method of determination; or require the passage of members between tellers, and their count, as the sole test; or the count of the speaker or the clerk, and an announcement from the desk of the names of those who are present. Any one of these methods, it must be conceded, is reasonably certain of ascertaining the fact; and as there is no constitutional method prescribed, and no constitutional inhibition of any of those, and no violation of fundamental rights in any, it follows that the house may adopt either or all, or it may provide for a combination of any two of the methods. That was done by the rule in question, and all that that rule attempts to do is to prescribe the method for ascertaining the presence of a maj0rity, and thus establishing the fact that the house is in a condition to transact business.[38]

Ch. 5, The People's Solution

While this case did not concern a Senate rule of procedure, it did concern the right of either house to determine its own rules of procedure and did set forth that such rules can not violate fundamental rights or any constitutional inhibitions. If not considered a direct precedent it is very close, and the closest one we have found and supportive of abolishing Senate procedures requiring a super majority or blocking some equal representation in debate in the Senate, except where specifically authorized by the Constitution, as violation of the equal representation of every State and every Senator.

Chapter 6, What You Can Do.

It is clear as it has been for the last hundred years that the means are present to remove the super majority rules that protect a small oligarchy in the United States Senate and those special interests that they represent. It is also absolutely clear after almost 100 years, since 1917, that we the people cannot depend upon our Senators to correct these blatant constitutional violations and return the rule of one Senator, one vote, to the United States Senate. They either cannot or will not reform their practices requiring super majorities and allowing minorities and even individual Senators to unreasonably delay the business of the Nation, except in the most minor ways and to continue to ignore their sworn duties to the States and the people of those States.

Organize, Educate and Inform the Public.

Change requires an informed public. So long as this information remains the property of just a select few, little change can be expected. You can start to inform the public by making sure this information is available to every civics class, every library, every public interest and talk show host and media personality, every politician from dog catcher to your Senator, court personnel and judges of all levels, every civic's teacher, every law school professor and constitutional

Ch. 6, What You Can Do.

law class, every public interest law firm, every public interest forum and town meeting, all of your neighbors, your church and other religious organizations with interest in the public good and public affairs. Anyone you feel has an interest in public affairs should have a copy of this work so that they may be informed.

Change may require a bit of personal sacrifice, as each reader my feel that he or she has been protected by one or more successful filibusters. But can any of you readers say this has been the case in all these actions and should these personal satisfactions outweigh the clear language of the Constitution? Where are your principles?

Change will only come through public demand as it is in various special interests groups to keep this information quiet and preserve their narrow aims through reducing the number of Senators they need to influence to pass any authorization or legislation or block any legislation. This is a major fight to take your country back and the people need to be armed with the ammunition, this information, to do it. It is up to you to help arm the people. I have done my part in writing this book. You do yours by organizing, petitioning and spreading the word.

Notes

1. Max Ferrand, Records of the Federal Convention of 1787, 11:94 Monday, July 23, James H. Hutson, editor ©1987. This was carried over to the committee in detail II:133, 141, 154, 165, 179, 232-234, 243,, 566, 591.

2. The Federalist, Edward Gaylord Bourne, editor, 1901, I:423.

3. One excellent article provides much of the history recited here, in further depth: Martin H. Gold & Dimple Gupta; The Constitutional Option to Change Senate Rules and Procedures: A Majoritarian Means to Over Come the Filibuster, 28 Harv. J.L. & Pub. Pol'y 205

4. Martin H. Gold & Dimple Gupta; The Constitutional Option to Change Senate Rules and Procedures: A Majoritarian Means to Over Come the Filibuster, 28 Harv. J.L. & Pub. Pol'y 229

5. 1959 Cong. Q. Almanac 213.

6. See 111 Cong. Rec: 3850 [1975] ("List of Cloture Votes Since Adoption of Rule 22")

7. Senator Thurmond switched parties in 1964 and remained a Republican until his death in 2003. He had been a Democrat from 1956 to 1964.

8. Brian Beutler | January 28, 2011, TPMDC
http://tpmdc.talkingpointsmemo.com/2011/01/to
m-harkin-looks-to-courts-to-reform-the-filibuster
.php#more

9. Brian Beutler | January 28, 2011 TPMDC,
http://tpmdc.talkingpointsmemo.com/2011/01/to
m-harkin-looks-to-courts-to-reform-the-filibuster
.php#more

10. Senate Cloture Rule, S.Rep. 99-95, at 15
(1985)

11. Franklin L. Burdette: *Filibustering in The
Senate* (1940) note 24 at 56.

12. 123 CONG. REC. 31,916 (statement of Sen.
Byrd) (1977)

13. *id.* at 31,919 (statement of Vice President
Mondale).

14. id. at 31,916 (statement of Sen. Abourezk)

15. *id.* at 31,919

16. *id.* at 31-919-20.

17. *id.* at 31,927-28 (1977)

18. 126 CONG. REC. 4729 (1980) (Senator
Byrd)

19. *id.* (Statement of Sen. Helms)

20. *Id.* at 4730 (statement of Sen. Byrd)

21. *Id.* (Statement of Sen. McClure)

22. *Id.* at 4732.

23. 125 CONG. REC. 31,877 - 93 (1979).

24. 133 CONG. REC. 12,252 - 59 (1987).

25. *Id.* at 12,258 (statement of Sen. Simpson).

26. Martin H. Gold & Dimple Gupta; The Constitutional Option to Change Senate Rules and Procedures: A Majoritarian Means to Over Come the Filibuster, 28 Harv. J.L. & Pub. Pol'y 270 n. 424.

27. *Id.*

28. *Muskrat v. United States*, 219 U.S. 346 (1911).

29. *Frothingham v. Mellon*, 262 U.S. 47 (1923).

30. 354 F. 2d 608 (2nd Cir., 1965), cert. Denied, 384 U.S. 941 (1966).

31. 397 U.S. 150, 152 (1970).

32. 412 U.S. 669 (1973).

33. 120 S.Ct. 693 (2000) reversed and remanded, 149 F.3d 303 (4th Cir. 1998).

34. 504 U.S. 555 at 560 (1992).

35. 144 U.S. 1 (1892).

36. *Id*. at 5

37. *Id*. at 5, 6

38. *Id*. at 6.

www.ingramcontent.com/pod-product-compliance
Lightning Source LLC
Chambersburg PA
CBHW022128280326
41933CB00007B/598